WHAT CAN AN Animal Do?

I Wonder Why

WHAT CAN AN
Animal
Do?

By Lawrence F. Lowery

Illustrated by Jan Ploog

NSTA **Kids**
National Science Teachers Association
Arlington, Virginia

National Science Teachers Association

Claire Reinburg, Director
Jennifer Horak, Managing Editor
Andrew Cooke, Senior Editor
Wendy Rubin, Associate Editor
Agnes Bannigan, Associate Editor
Amy America, Book Acquisitions Coordinator

ART AND DESIGN
Will Thomas Jr., Director
Joe Butera, Cover, Interior Design
Original illustrations by Jan Pfloog

PRINTING AND PRODUCTION
Catherine Lorrain, Director

NATIONAL SCIENCE TEACHERS ASSOCIATION
Gerald F. Wheeler, Executive Director
David Beacom, Publisher

1840 Wilson Blvd., Arlington, VA 22201
www.nsta.org/store
For customer service inquiries, please call 800-277-5300.

Lexile® measure: 150L

Library of Congress Cataloging-in-Publication Data
Lowery, Lawrence F.
  What can an animal do? / by Lawrence F. Lowery ; illustrated by Jan Pfloog.
    p. cm. -- (I wonder why)
  Originally published: New York : Holt, Rinehart and Winston, 1969.
  ISBN 978-1-936959-45-7
  1. Animals--Juvenile literature. 2. Animal behavior--Juvenile literature. I. Pfloog, Jan, ill. II. Title.
  QL49.L9 2012
  591.5--dc23
                        2012026552

eISBN 978-1-936959-58-7

Introduction

The *I Wonder Why* books are science books created specifically for young learners who are in their first years of school. The content for each book was chosen to be appropriate for youngsters who are beginning to construct knowledge of the world around them. These youngsters ask questions. They want to know about things. They are more curious than when they are a decade older. Research shows that science is these students' favorite subject when they enter school for the first time.

Science is both *what* we know and *how* we come to know it. What we know is the content knowledge that accumulates over time as scientists continue to explore the universe in which we live. How we come to know science is the set of thinking and reasoning processes humans use to get answers to the questions and inquiries in which we are engaged.

Scientists learn by observing, comparing, and organizing. So do children. These thinking processes are among several inquiry behaviors that enable us to find out about our world and how it works. Observing, comparing, and organizing are fundamental to the more advanced processes of relating, experimenting, and inferring.

The five books in this set of the *I Wonder Why* series focus on inquiry and various content topics: animal behavior, plant growth, physical characteristics of sound, animal adaptations, and mathematical measurement. Inquiry is a natural human attribute initiated by curiosity. When we don't know something about an area of our interest, we try to understand by asking questions and by doing. The five books are titled by questions children may ask: *How Does a Plant Grow? What Can an Animal Do? What Does an Animal Eat?*

What Makes Different Sounds? and *How Tall Was Milton?* Children inquire about plants, animals, and other phenomena. Their curiosity leads them to ask about measurements, the growth of plants, the characteristics of sounds, what animals eat, and how animals behave. The inquiries lead the characters in the books and the reader to discover the need for standard measures, the characteristics of plant growth, sound, and animal adaptations.

Each book uses a different approach to take the reader through simple scientific information from a child's point of view: One book is a narrative, another is expository. One book uses poetry, another presents ideas through a fairy tale. In addition, the illustrations display different artistic styles to help convey information. Some art is fantasy, some realistic. Some art is bright and abstract, some pastel and whimsical. The combining of art, literary techniques, and scientific knowledge brings the content to the reader through several instructional avenues.

In addition, the content in these books correlates to criteria set forth by national standards. Often the content is woven into each book so that its presence is subtle but powerful. The science activities in the Parent/Teacher Handbook section within each book enable students to carry out their own investigations that relate to the content of the book. The materials needed for these activities are easily obtained, and the activities have been tested with youngsters to be sure they are age appropriate.

After students have completed a science activity, rereading or referring back to the book and talking about connections with the activity is a deepening experience that stabilizes the learning as a long-term memory.

What, oh what, can a jackrabbit do?

It can run.

It can hop.

It can nibble on a carrot.

That is what the jackrabbit can do.

What do you think a cute kitten can do?

It can purr.

It can sleep.

It can lick its soft fur.

That is what the kitten can do.

What, oh what, can a puppy dog do?

It can bark.

It can dig.

It can wag its friendly tail.

That is what the puppy can do.

Do you know what a strong horse can do?

It can trot.

It can gallop.

It can take you for a ride.

That is what the horse can do.

What, oh what, can a brown beaver do?

It can gnaw.

It can swim.

It can build a house dam.

That is what the beaver can do.

What do you think a grown pig can do?

It can oink.

It can squeal.

It can wallow in the mud.

That is what the pig can do.

What, oh what, can a dark spider do?

It can spin a web.

It can catch a fly.

It can climb a tall wall.

That is what the spider can do.

Do you know what a grasshopper can do?

It can jump.

It can fly.

It can eat lots of plants.

That is what the grasshopper can do.

What, oh what, can a little bird do?

It can eat seeds.

It can sing.

It can fly with its wings.

That is what the bird can do.

What do you think a green turtle can do?

It can crawl.

It can swim.

It can hide in its shell.

That is what the turtle can do.

What, oh what, can a feathered duck do?

It can waddle.

It can float.

It can fly in the sky.

That is what the duck can do.

What, oh what, can a bumblebee do?

It can buzz.

It can sting.

It can gather nectar to make honey.

That is what the bumblebee can do.

What do you think a bullfrog can do?

It can croak.

It can jump.

It can splash in the water.

That is what the bullfrog can do.

What, oh what, can a giant whale do?

It can swim.

It can dive.

It can upend a boat.

That is what the whale can do.

What do you think a kangaroo can do?

It can hop.

It can leap.

It can carry babies in its pouch.

That is what the roo can do.

What do you think a tiger can do?

It can growl.

It can run.

It can lick its soft fur.

That is what the tiger can do.

Do you know what a sea crab can do?

It can swim.

It can pinch.

It can skitter sideways.

That is what the sea crab can do.

What, oh what, can a caterpillar do?

It can crawl.

It can sleep.

It can change to a butterfly.

That is what the caterpillar can do.

What, oh what, can a tiny fish do?

It can swim.

It can blow bubbles.

It can eat seaweed too.

That is what the fish can do.

What, oh what, can you do that other animals cannot do?

Can you play a piano?   Can you multiply and divide?

Can you read a book?   Can you knit a warm sweater?

Can you use a computer?   Can you laugh at a joke?

Do you know how to cook?   Can you write a long letter?

What else can you do that other animals cannot do?

WHAT CAN AN
Animal Do?

Parent/Teacher Handbook

Introduction

What Can an Animal Do? asks questions about certain animals and their distinctive behaviors. This book uses inquiry as its structure and serves to introduce readers to the basic processes of science: observing, comparing, and communicating (by describing).

Inquiry Processes

Careful observation is very important to scientists. This book, for beginning readers and young scientists, is designed to engage its audience in observing and thinking about experiences. The selected animals show a variety of characteristics and behaviors to help learners become familiar with a variety of descriptive words and images. Subtle parallels, such as between the kitten and the tiger, provide opportunities for the alert youngster to participate in observation and insight.

Each animal is introduced through a carefully and clearly drawn illustration supplemented by a simple repetitively structured text from which the child gains a measure of familiarity with the animal's characteristics (size, shape, color, etc.) and its actions (flying, running, swimming, etc.).

The text guides the child's observations and thoughts to particular aspects of behavior, then ends with an open-ended question that asks the child to compare the behaviors of animals to his or her own behaviors.

CARNIVORA

Felidae: Angora, Persian, Siamese, Manx

Ursidae: Polar, Grizzly, Kodiak

Canidae: Beagle, Terrier, Poodle, Setter, Spaniel

Content

Animals are identified by their characteristics (e.g., size, shape, color) and behaviors (e.g., jump, hop, slither). Comparisons of animals based on similarities and differences enable scientists to group animals by commonalities of characteristics. For example, lions, tigers, panthers, and domestic cats have some common characteristics by which they can be grouped together. Scientists call this super ordinate grouping the *Felidae* family. Similarly, the dog family, called the *Canidae* family, is made up of wolves, foxes, spaniels, terriers, and more. The bear family is called the *Ursidae* family and includes polar, grizzly, and kodiak bears.

It is important to distinguish animals by characteristics to better understand how different-looking animals are part of a larger group of related animals.

Science Activities

Observing Animal Behaviors

A terrarium is a miniature environment with living plants and small animals. A terrarium is a great way to observe the behaviors of some small animals in a setting that represents where they live. A pet store can provide information on how to set up a dry (desert) or wet (swamp) terrarium. For each animal you plan to observe, follow the guidelines for food, lighting, temperature, types of plants, and other factors. When set up properly, the environment will be nearly self-sustaining. You will just need to check water and clean up any debris.

The types of small animals that can be observed in a terrarium are caterpillars, chameleons, crickets, earthworms, frogs, geckos, grasshoppers, iguanas, land snails, newts, salamanders, snakes, sow bugs, tadpoles, toads, and turtles.

The housing and care for larger animals require some research and special handling. Information on the housing, feeding, and care of the animal can be obtained at most pet stores or through internet research.

Note: *Both large and small animals should be cared for properly. Be careful not to hurt or harm them in any way.*

Examples for Observing an Animal's Behavior

Here are examples of ways to observe the behavior of a small animal. These examples can serve as suggestions for observing the behavior of other animals, too.

1. Place several land snails in a properly prepared terrarium with green leaves. Cover it with a piece of nylon stocking to keep the snails from climbing out of the container.

   a. Observe how the land snails move.

   b. Observe how they find food and eat.

   c. Gently touch the eyes of a snail at the ends of its extended stalks with a feather. Observe what the snail does. Touch it gently in various other places and observe what happens. If the snail is overly disturbed, it will retreat into its shell.

   d. Place two snails near each other but facing in opposite directions. Ring a small bell or click a cricket clicker and observe the behavior of the snails. Do the animals respond to the sound? Use the observations to answer the question, "Why were the snails placed facing in opposite directions?" This observational experiment can be done with other animals, too.

   e. Place an upright board in the terrarium. Observe whether or not snails always climb upward. When a snail reaches the top of the board, turn the board over and observe what it does. Try tipping the board at different angles to observe what effect the angle of tilt has on the direction in which the snail travels.

   f. Prepare another board with four holes in it. One hole should be able to easily accommodate the snail's shell. The smaller holes should accommodate the snail's body, but not the shell. Place the board in the path of a snail and see how it is able to select the right-size hole through which to travel.

   g. Design a test to see if snails move toward or away from a heat or light source.

2. Place other animals in appropriate environments (grasshoppers, caterpillars, earthworms, hamsters, and so on). Feed them properly, and observe what, when, and how each eats. Watch how they move. When do they sleep? Do they respond to sounds you make?